Operation Code

Scratch 3.0

Coding at the Grocery Store

D1709681

By Colleen van Lent and Kristin Fontichiaro

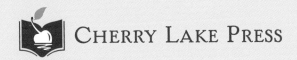
CHERRY LAKE PRESS

Published in the United States of America by Cherry Lake Publishing
Ann Arbor, Michigan
www.cherrylakepublishing.com

Series Adviser: Kristin Fontichiaro
Reading Adviser: Marla Conn, MS, Ed., Literacy specialist, Read-Ability, Inc.

Image Credits: ©Clker-Free-Vector-Images/Pixabay, 6, 10, 14, 16, 20; Maze image courtesy of Kristin Fontichiaro and Colleen van Lent, 6, 10, 14, 16, 20; ©AnnaliseArt/Pixabay, 4; ©Viscious-Speed/Pixabay, 4; ©OpenClipart-Vectors/Pixabay, 6, 10, 14, 16, 20; ©burhankhawaja/Pixabay, 6, 10, 14, 16, 20; Various images throughout courtesy of Scratch

Library of Congress Cataloging-in-Publication Data

Names: van Lent, Colleen, author. | Fontichiaro, Kristin, author.
Title: Coding at the grocery store / by Colleen Van Lent and Kristin Fontichiaro.
Description: Ann Arbor, Michigan : Cherry Lake Publishing, 2020. | Series: Operation code | Includes index. | Audience: Grades 2-3.
Identifiers: LCCN 2019035737 (print) | LCCN 2019035738 (ebook) | ISBN 9781534159297 (hardcover) | ISBN 9781534161597 (paperback) |
   ISBN 9781534160446 (pdf) | ISBN 9781534162747 (ebook)
Subjects: LCSH: Scratch (Computer program language)—Juvenile literature. | Computer programming—Juvenile literature. | Grocery shopping—
   Computer simulation—Juvenile literature.
Classification: LCC QA76.73.S345 V3567 2020 (print) | LCC QA76.73.S345 (ebook) | DDC 005.13/3—dc23
LC record available at https://lccn.loc.gov/2019035737
LC ebook record available at https://lccn.loc.gov/2019035738

Cherry Lake Publishing would like to acknowledge the work of the Partnership for 21st Century Learning, a Network of Battelle for Kids.
Please visit http://www.battelleforkids.org/networks/p21 for more information.

Printed in the United States of America
Corporate Graphics

NOTE TO READERS: Use this book to practice your Scratch 3 coding skills. If you have never used Scratch before, ask a parent, teacher, or librarian to help you set up an account at *https://scratch.mit.edu*. Read the tutorials on the website to learn how Scratch works. Then you will be ready for the activities in this book! You will practice using variables, if/then statements, copying code to other sprites, using effects to change a sprite's look, and more! Find all the starter and final programs at *https://scratch.mit.edu/users/CherryLakeCoding*.

Table of Contents

Let's Play!

Welcome to the grocery store game! You have 30 seconds to move a shopping cart using the arrow keys. You get 1 point for each piece of fruit you touch. You get 10 points for reaching the cash register before time runs out.

Pro Tip!

Scratch lets you see other people's projects and copy them to make them your own. Our code contains the **sprites**, backdrops, and sounds we will use in this book. You will be adding more!

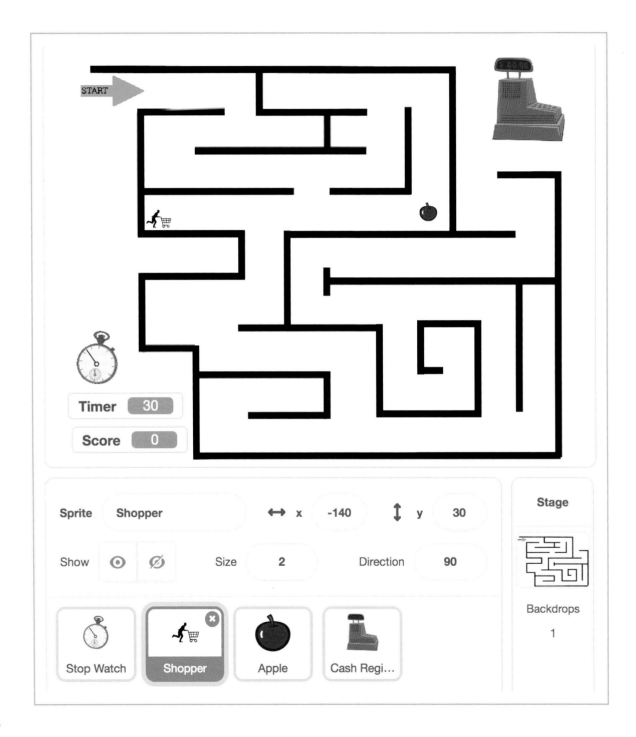

6

Keeping Time and Score

The Stop Watch sprite has a lot of great code. It controls a timer that ends the game after 30 seconds. It also has some cool sound effects. The code for the cash register is all set too! You won't need to change them.

Play the game made so far. You can find it at *https://scratch.mit.edu/projects/312091140*.

Pro Tip!

The maze is not a **default** background. We drew and **uploaded** our own image. We also added the Stop Watch, Shopper, and Cash Register sprites.

Popular Sensing Blocks

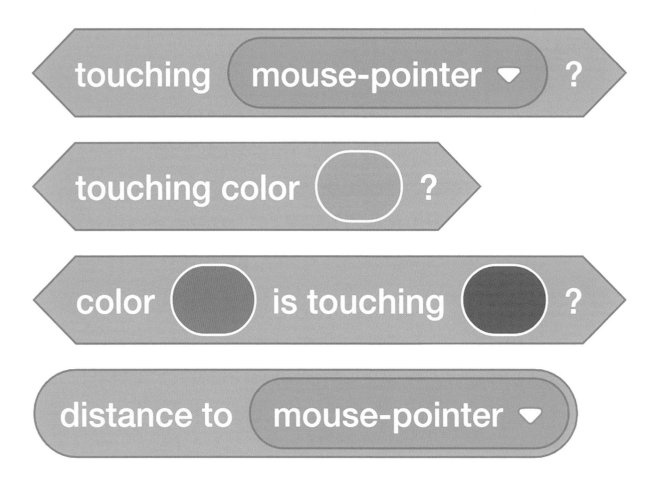

touching mouse-pointer ▼ ?

touching color ?

color is touching ?

distance to mouse-pointer ▼

Debugging the Program

Did you notice anything wrong? The shopping cart can go through walls! Someone might cheat if we don't fix that.

Let's think about ways we can fix the **bug**. Look at the Sensing blocks for ideas on fixing this problem.

Pro Tip!

These popular Sensing blocks can be adjusted. Blocks can be changed. Your sprite can check for the mouse-pointer, or it can sense if it is touching another sprite. You can also change the blocks to "sense" for a different color.

How to Select the Right Color for Your Sensing Block

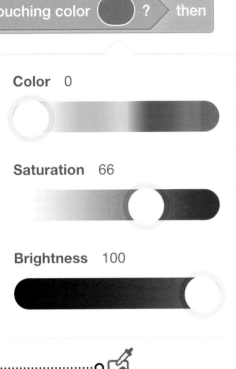

Step 1: Add *touching color* to the **if ... then** block. Click on the colored circle.

Step 2: Click the eyedropper tool.

Step 3: Drag the mouse over the maze until you see the wall color in the middle of the circle. Then click.

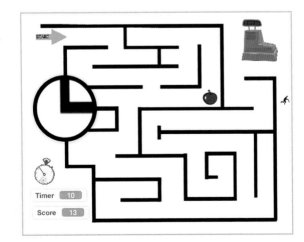

Watch Those Walls!

How can I keep the sprite from running into a wall? Time to problem solve.

You can't tell Scratch to avoid hitting walls, but you can tell it to take action if it touches a certain color, like the black part of the wall. Click on the Shopper sprite.

Add this Control block:

Then follow the steps on page 10.

Pro Tip!

Most video games require the computer to sense, or pay attention to certain things, like the background or other sprites. Can you think of a computer or video game that does this?

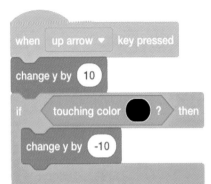

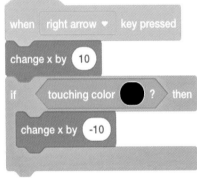

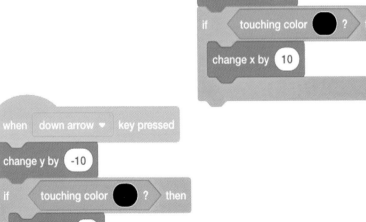

12

Bouncing Back

The starter code moves the cart 10 steps when you press an arrow key. Now that we know how to **detect** colors, let's code what happens when you touch a wall.

If the shopping cart touches a wall, change the x or y to go back to where it just was. You can find the `change x by ◯` and `change y by ◯` blocks under Motion.

Pro Tip!

Always check for **logic errors**. For right and left, you change x. For up and down, you change y. Remember, positive numbers will always move your sprite up or to the right. Negative numbers will always move your sprite down or to the left.

Adjust size of sprite

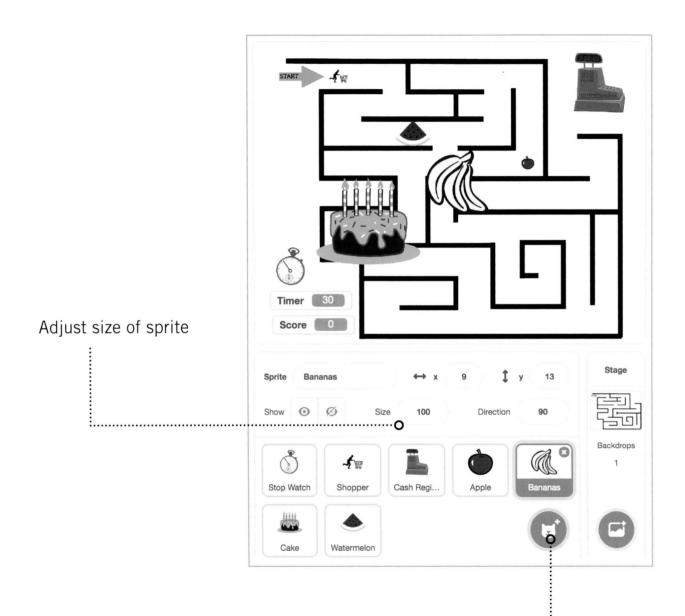

Find more sprites

Adding More Fruit (and Cake!)

We need more food sprites so players can earn more points! Scratch has many sprites you can choose from in its built-in library.

We had to shrink the Apple sprite to make it fit in the maze. You will have to do the same with your sprites. For example, we changed the size of the Bananas sprite to 30.

Pro Tip!

When you want a certain kind of sprite, use the **categories** at the top of the sprite library. Try the Food category!

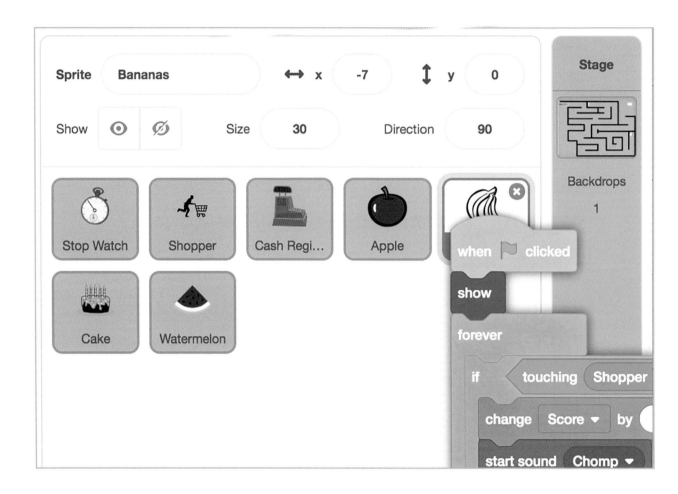

Sprite Bananas ↔ x -7 ↕ y 0

Show ⊙ ⊘ Size 30 Direction 90

Stop Watch

Shopper

Cash Regi...

Apple

Cake

Watermelon

when ⚑ clicked

show

forever

if touching Shopper

change Score ▾ by

start sound Chomp ▾

Stage

Backdrops

1

16

Coding the Smart Way

We want all of the food to have the same code as the Apple sprite. You don't have to write it again. You can copy the code from the Apple sprite.

To do that, click on the Apple sprite. Then click and drag its code on top of the sprite you want to receive the code.

Pro Tip!

When you drag the code to a new sprite, you will see the sprite "wiggle" for a second. Sometimes it takes one or two tries. Don't worry if the code disappears from the scripts area while you are dragging it. The code will reappear when you release your mouse.

Little Changes

Click on each new food and make sure that you copied the code. Test out the game.

Want an extra challenge? Change the sound for some of the sprites. How about a "glug" for the Milk sprite or the "birthday" song for the cake? To choose a new sound, click the Sounds tab. Then click the Choose a Sound option at the bottom left.

Pro Tip!
You can change any sound by making it faster, slower, or even reversing it! The ✂ tool will cut off parts you don't want at all.

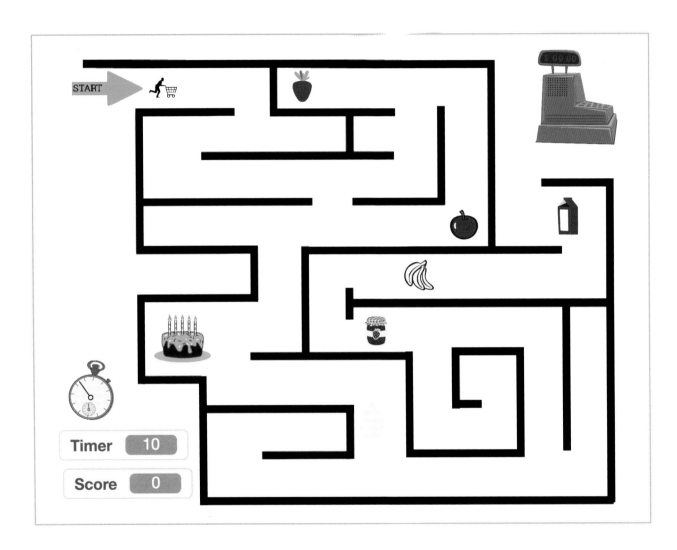

Play Your Game!

Test your game and then challenge your friends!

Want to make your game more challenging? Here are a few ideas:

- Subtract points for foods you don't like.

- Change the background when you win or lose.

What other ideas do you have?

Pro Tip!
If you would like to see our final code, go to
https://scratch.mit.edu/projects/309591006.

Glossary

bug (BUHG) a mistake in your code

categories (KAT-uh-gor-eez) groups of things that have something in common

default (DEE-fawlt) the choice Scratch makes for you in advance that you can change

detect (dih-TEKT) to sense or identify something

if ... then (IF THEN) a block that says, "IF (this thing) is true, THEN (this thing) will happen"

logic errors (LAH-jik ER-urz) mistakes in your code that will make it run weirdly

sprites (SPRYTS) characters or objects in Scratch

uploaded (UHP-lohd-id) copied a file from your computer to Scratch, the Web, or another software

Find Out More

Books

LEAD Project. *Super Scratch Programming Adventure!* San Francisco, California: No Starch Press, 2012.

Lovett, Amber. *Coding with Blockly.* Ann Arbor, Michigan: Cherry Lake Publishing, 2017.

Ziter, Rachel. *Coding Games from Scratch: An Augmented Reading Experience.* North Mankato, Minnesota: Capstone Press, 2019.

Websites

Scratch
https://scratch.mit.edu
Get started with Scratch at this website.

Scratch Wiki: Variable
https://en.scratch-wiki.info/wiki/Variable
Learn more about variables from the Scratch team.

Index

About the Authors

Colleen van Lent teaches coding and Web design at the University of Michigan School of Information. She has three cool kids and a dog named Bacon. She wishes she could touch her toes.

Kristin Fontichiaro teaches at the University of Michigan School of Information. She likes working with kids on creative projects from coding to sewing to junk box inventions. She has written or edited almost 100 books for kids.